Sophocles
Ajax

Translated by
Ian Johnston
Vancouver Island University
Nanaimo, BC
Canada

Richer Resources Publications
Arlington, Virginia
USA

Sophocles
Ajax

Cover Art by Ian Crowe

Richer Resources Publications
1926 N. Woodrow Street
Arlington, Virginia 22207

Or via our web site at
www.RicherResourcesPublications.com

ISBN 978-1-935238-93-5
Library of Congress Control Number: 2010922349

Published by Richer Resources Publications
Arlington, Virginia.
Printed in the United States of America.

Sophocles
Ajax

Translator's Note

In numbering the lines in the following English text, the translator has normally included short indented lines with the short line immediately above it, so that the two partial lines count as a single line in the reckoning. The line numbers in square brackets refer to the Greek text. Explanatory footnotes have been added by the translator.

The translator would like to acknowledge the extremely valuable help of W. B. Stanford's commentary on the play and of the translation of Sir Richard Jebb.

Introductory Note

When Achilles, the finest of all the warriors in the Achaean army, was killed in the Trojan War, there was a dispute about which warrior should receive the high honour of getting Achilles' weapons. There were two main claimants, Odysseus and Ajax. The latter was, according to Homer, the finest warrior after Achilles. However, as a result of voting among the leading warriors, the weapons were awarded to Odysseus. The action of Sophocles' play takes place the day after this decision.

Note that Sophocles calls the Greek forces the Argives, Achaeans, or Danaans, as in Homer, and occasionally the Hellenes (Greeks).

Sophocles (c. 496 BC to 406 BC) was one of the greatest of the ancient Greek tragic dramatists. Only seven of his more than one hundred and twenty plays survive. The exact date for the first production of Ajax is unknown, but it is widely assumed to be one of his earlier works (c. 440 BC).

Ajax
Dramatis Personae

ATHENA: goddess of war and wisdom
ODYSSEUS: king of Ithaca, a leader in the Argive forces at Troy
AJAX: king of Salamis
CHORUS: sailors from Salamis
TECMESSA: daughter of the king of Phrygia, concubine of Ajax
MESSENGER: a soldier
TEUCER: a Greek warrior, half-brother of Ajax
MENELAUS: one of the commanders of the Argive forces at Troy
AGAMEMNON: brother of Menelaus, commander of the Greeks
EURYSACES: young son of Ajax and Tecmessa.
ATTENDANTS, SERVANTS, SOLDIERS

[The action takes place during the last year of the Trojan War. The scene is one end of the Argive camp beside the sea, outside Ajax's hut. The hut is a substantial building with main doors facing the audience and some side doors. There are steps leading up to a platform outside the main doors. It is early in the morning, without very much light yet. ODYSSEUS enters slowly, tracking footprints in the sand and trying to look through the partially open door into the hut. The goddess ATHENA appears and speaks to ODYSSEUS.]

ATHENA
    Odysseus, I keep seeing you prowl around,
    seeking by stealth to gain the upper hand
    against your enemies. And now, by these huts
    at one end of the army, where Ajax
    has his camp beside the ships, for some time
    I've been observing as you track him down,
    keeping your eyes fixed on his fresh-made trail,
    to find out whether he's inside or not.[1]
    Like a keen-nosed Spartan hunting dog
    your path is taking you straight to your goal—   10

---

[1]According to Homer, Ajax's encampment lay at one end of the Argive line, a position more exposed than other parts and hence a mark of Ajax's courage. Achilles' encampment was at the other end. The phrase "of the army" has been added to clarify this point.

the man has just gone in, his head and arms
dripping with sweat after the butchery   [10]
he's just carried out with his own sword.
So you don't need to peer inside the doors.
What are you so eager to discover here?
Why not tell me? You could learn the answer
from someone who knows.

ODYSSEUS *[looking up but he cannot see Athena]*
                    Ah, Athena's voice, of the gods
the one I cherish most. How clear you sound.
I can't see you, but I do hear your words—
my mind can grasp their sense, like the bronze call   20
of an Etruscan trumpet.[1] And you are right.
You see me circling around, tracking down
that man who hates me, shield-bearing Ajax.
I've been following his trail a long time now—   [20]
just him, no one else. During the night
he's done something inconceivable to us,
if he's the one who did it. We're not sure.
We don't know anything for certain.
So I volunteered to find out what's gone on.
We've just discovered all our livestock killed—   30
our plunder butchered by some human hand,
and with them the men who guard the herd.
Everyone blames Ajax for the slaughter.
What's more, an eyewitness who saw him
striding by himself across the plain, his sword   [30]
dripping with fresh blood, informed me of it
and told me what he saw. I ran off at once
to pick up his trail. I'm following the tracks.
But it's confusing—sometimes I don't know
whose prints they are. So you've come just in time,   40

[1]These lines make clear that Odysseus cannot, at this point, see Athena, either
because it is still too dark or because she has concealed herself somewhere (or
both). Given what happens in a moment, it is not feasible that Athena is simply a
disembodied voice.

for in the past and in the days to come
your hand has been and will remain my guide.

ATHENA
I am aware of that, Odysseus, that's why
for some time I've been keen to come to you
as a watchman on your hunt.

ODYSSEUS
Well then, dear lady,
will what I'm doing here have good results?

ATHENA
I'll tell you this: Ajax did those killings,
as you suspected.

ODYSSEUS
Why would he do that?   [40]
Why turn his hands to such a senseless act?

ATHENA
The weapons—that armour from Achilles—   50
it made him insanely angry.[1]

ODYSSEUS
But then
why would he slaughter all the animals?

ATHENA
He thought he was staining both his hands
with blood from you.

ODYSSEUS
You mean this was his plan
against the Argives?

[1] When Achilles, the greatest fighter among the Argive leaders, was killed (shortly
before the action of this play) his divinely made armour was set up as a prestigious
prize among the Argive warriors. Odysseus and Ajax were the main claimants, and
as the result of a vote among the Argive leaders, the weapons were awarded to
Odysseus, over the strong objections of Ajax, who, according to was considered the
finest Argive warrior after Achilles.

ATHENA

          Yes—and it would have worked,
if I had not been paying attention.

ODYSSEUS

    How could he have done something so reckless?
How could his mind have been so rash?

ATHENA

                    At night
in secret he crept out alone after you.

ODYSSEUS

    How close was he? Did he get to his target?   60

ATHENA

    He reached the camp of both commanders—
he made it right up to their double gates.[1]

ODYSSEUS

    If he was so insanely keen for slaughter,   [50]
how could he prevent his hands from killing?

ATHENA

    I stopped him. I threw down into his eyes
an overwhelming sense of murderous joy
and turned his rage against the sheep and cattle
and those protecting them—the common herd
which so far has not been divided up.[2]
He launched his attack against those animals   70
and kept on chopping down and slaughtering
the ones with horns by slicing through their spines,
until they made a circle all around him.
At one point he thought he was butchering
both sons of Atreus—he had them in his hands.
Then he went at some other general

---

[1]The two commanders are Agamemnon and Menelaus, sons of Atreus and the chief leaders of the Argive forces at Troy.

[2]This detail means that Ajax has killed animals belonging to everyone, since all soldiers were to receive some of the cattle or sheep as battle spoils.

8

and then another. As he charged around
in his sick frenzy, I kept encouraging him,
kept pushing him into those fatal nets.   [60]
And then, when he took a rest from killing,   80
he tied up the sheep and cattle still alive
and led them home, as if he had captured
human prisoners and not just animals.
Now he keeps them tied up in his hut
and tortures them. I'll let you see his madness—
in plain view here—so you can witness it
and then report to all the Argives. Be brave.
Do not back off or look upon this man
as any threat to you. I will avert his eyes,
so he will never see your face.   [70]

[Calling to Ajax inside the hut]

                            You in there—   90
the one who's tying up his prisoner's arms—
I'm calling you! I'm shouting now for Ajax!
Come on out here! Outside the hut! In front!

ODYSSEUS
Athena! What are you doing? Don't call him!
Don't bring him out here!

ATHENA
                        Just be patient.
Don't run the risk of being called a coward.

ODYSSEUS
For the gods' sake, don't do it! Leave him be!
Let him stay inside!

ATHENA
                    What's the matter with you?
He was just a man before this, wasn't he?

ODYSSEUS
Yes, and in the past unfriendly to me,   100
and especially now.

9

ATHENA
>But the sweetest laughter
comes from mocking enemies. Is that not true?

ODYSSEUS
Still, I'd prefer he stayed inside his hut. [80]

ATHENA
You hesitate to see before your eyes
someone in a raving fit?

ODYSSEUS
>Yes, I do—
if he were fully sane I'd not avoid him
or hesitate . . .

ATHENA
>But he won't see you now,
not even if you stand beside him.

ODYSSEUS
How will that occur, if he still can see
with his own eyes?

ATHENA
>His eyes see very well, 110
but I will make them dark.

ODYSSEUS
>Well, it is true
a god's work can make all things possible.

ATHENA
Stand here, then, and stay quiet.

ODYSSEUS
>I'd better stay,
although I'd have preferred to keep my distance.

ATHENA
You in there, Ajax! I'm calling you again!
Why show your ally so much disrespect? [90]

[AJAX enters from the hut. He is carrying a bloody whip with which he has been lashing the cattle]

AJAX

Welcome Athena! Welcome child of Zeus!
You have given me so much assistance![1]
In gratitude for those I've captured
I'll offer you a crown, presents of pure gold.   120

ATHENA

That's nobly spoken. But tell me this—
did that sword of yours slake itself on blood
when you attacked the Argive army?

AJAX

                                        Yes.
That I can boast about. I don't deny it.

ATHENA

You went after the two sons of Atreus
with that weapon in your fist?

AJAX

                                        Indeed I did.
They'll not dishonour Ajax any more.

ATHENA

So, as I understand you, those men are dead.

AJAX

Yes, dead. Let them rob me of my weapons now!   [100]

ATHENA

I see. Well, what about Laertes' son?[2]   130
As far as you're concerned, where does he stand?
Did he escape you?

---

[1]In Homer's *Iliad*, Athena consistently supports the Argives, including Ajax, during the Trojan War.
[2]Laertes' son is Odysseus.

AJAX

That damned slimy fox!
You ask me where he is?

ATHENA

Yes, I'm asking.
I mean that enemy of yours, Odysseus.

AJAX

My favourite prisoner, lady, sits inside.
I don't want him to die just yet.

ATHENA

But when?
What further actions do you have to do?
Or what advantage will you gain by that?

AJAX

Not before he's tied up to a pillar,
the main one holding up the roof in there.   140

ATHENA

What harm will you inflict on the poor man?

AJAX

I'll whip his back blood red. Then I'll kill him.   [110]

ATHENA

Don't abuse the poor man so viciously.

AJAX

You can follow your desires, Athena,
in all other things. That I will concede.
But this is the penalty he's going to pay—
not something else.

ATHENA

All right, since it pleases you,
give that arm of yours some exercise. Don't stop.
Do what you've planned.

AJAX

Then I'll get back to work.
And I'll leave you with this request from me—   150

always stand beside me as my ally
the way you did today.

[AJAX goes back into the hut]

ATHENA

                Do you see,
Odysseus, how powerful the gods can be?
Could you find anyone more sensible
than Ajax, a man with more ability
to carry out in every situation
the most appropriate action?   [120]

ODYSSEUS

               No one I know.
All the same, although he despises me,
I pity his misfortune under that yoke
of catastrophic madness. It makes me think   160
not just of his fate but my own as well.
I see that in our lives we are no more
than phantoms, insubstantial shadows.

ATHENA

Well then, now you've seen his arrogance,
make sure you never speak against the gods,
or give yourself ideas of your own grandeur,
if your strength of hand or heaped-up riches   [130]
should outweigh some other man's. A single day
pulls down any human's scale of fortune
or raises it once more. But the gods love   170
men who possess good sense and self-control
and despise the ones who are unjust.

[ATHENA and ODYSSEUS leave. Enter the CHORUS, sailors from
Salamis and followers of Ajax]

CHORUS LEADER

Son of Telamon, who holds the throne
on wave-washed Salamis beside the sea,
I rejoice with you when things go well,
but when a blow from Zeus or angry words
from slanderous Danaans are aimed at you,

13

then I hold back in fear and shake with terror,
like the fluttering eye on a feathered dove.   [140]
I'm like that now. In the night that's passing,   180
there were noisy rumours thrown against us,
against our honour, saying that you went off
into that meadow where our horses range
and massacred Danaan animals,
together with the spoils their spears had captured,
prizes which had not yet been allotted.
With that bright sword of yours you butchered them.
Such slanderous reports Odysseus shapes
and whispers into every soldier's ear.   [150]
Many men believe him. For he now speaks   190
persuasively about you, and everyone
who listens is filled with spite and pleased
that you have come to grief, even more
than is the man who told them. Throw a spear
at some great soul, and you will never miss,
but if someone said things like that of me,
he'd never be believed. Envy creeps up
against the man of wealth and power.
And yet without the great, we lesser men
are fragile ramparts in our own defence.   200
It's best for small men to ally themselves   [160]
with greatness, and for the powerful
to be supported by the lesser men.
But teaching foolish people such good sense
ahead of time is just not possible.
So men like this are now denouncing you,
and we do not possess sufficient power
to deflect these charges, not without you,
not without our king. With you out of their sight,
they keep on chattering like flocks of birds.   210
But if you unexpectedly appeared,
they would be terrified, as if they faced   [170]
a mighty eagle, and soon would cower there
and hold their tongues in silence.

CHORUS
Was it that goddess Artemis,

bull-tending child of Zeus,
who drove you on,
drove you at the common herd?
O mighty Rumour, mother of my shame!
Was it perhaps in retribution for a victory   220
where she received no tribute,
splendid weapons she was cheated of?
Or did some hunter kill a stag
and set no gifts aside for her?
Or has Enyalios, bronze-plated god of war,
with reason to complain about an armed alliance,
taken his revenge for such an insult   [180]
by a devious stratagem at night?

For with your own mind, O son of Telamon,
you'd never go so far along the path to ruin   230
as to attack the flocks. But nothing can prevent
a sickness which the gods implant.
I pray that Zeus, that Phoebus Apollo
will stave off this catastrophe,
this disastrous rumour of the Argives.
And if great kings are slandering you now
with stories full of lies, or if it is that man
born from the worthless line of Sisyphus,
do not, my lord, take on the grievous weight   [190]
of a dishonoured reputation by remaining here,   240
hiding your presence in this hut beside the sea.[1]

Up now, get up from where you sit,
wherever you've been settled for so long
in your pause from battle. You are fuelling
a fire of disaster blazing up to heaven.
Your enemies' insolence keeps charging on
quite fearlessly, whipped up by favouring winds
through forest thickets, while every soldier

[1]According to some legends Odysseus was the son of Sisyphus, a notoriously bad king of Corinth (rather than the son of Laertes, king of Ithaca, as in the *Odyssey*). This genealogy was a slur used by Odysseus' enemies. Later in the play, Teucer calls Odysseus "son of Laertes."

wags his tongue and laughs and jeers.
They bring us grief and reinforce our sorrow.   250   [200]

[Enter TECMESSA]

TECMESSA

You men, shipmates of Ajax, sons of the race
of earth-born Erechtheus, all of us
who love the distant house of Telamon
are in despair.[1] For now our master Ajax,
our great and terrifying and forceful king,
lies suffering from tempestuous disease.

CHORUS LEADER

What heavy grief has come during the night
to change the troubles we had yesterday?
Daughter of the Phrygian Teleutas,   [210]
speak to us—though bold Ajax won you   260
fighting with his spear, he still maintains
a strong affection for you, so you may know
and offer us an answer.

TECMESSA

                              How can I tell
a story much too terrifying for words?
You will hear of suffering as harsh as death.
Last night madness seized our glorious Ajax,
and now he has been totally disgraced.
You can see everything inside his hut,
the blood-soaked butchered victims who were killed
as sacrifices at his very hands.   270   [220]

CHORUS

The news you tell us of our fiery king
we cannot bear, yet there is no escape.
It's what the powerful Danaans say,

---

[1]Erechtheus was a legendary king of Athens who was born from the earth and thus gave the Athenians the claim that they were true natives of the land where they lived (autochthonous). Sophocles is here linking the sailors of Salamis with the residents of Athens (the audience). Salamis is an island just off the coast of Attica, the territory around and belonging to Athens.

what their great story-telling spreads around.
O, how I fear what's coming next. This man
is going to die—and in full public view—
with a black sword in those mad hands of his   [230]
he massacred the herd and herdsmen, too,
the ones who ride to guard our animals.

TECMESSA

Alas! From those fields he came to me   280
right after that, leading his captive beasts.
On the floor in there he slit some of their throats,
struck others in the ribs, tore them apart.
He grabbed two rams—the legs on both were white—
cut off the head on one and sliced its tongue,
right at the tip, then threw the parts away,
and lashed the other upright on the pillar.   [240]
He seized a thick strap from a horse's harness
and flogged it with a whistling double lash.
He was cursing with an awful violence,   290
not human words—ones a god had taught him.

CHORUS LEADER

The time has come for us to hide our heads
and steal away on foot—or take our seats,
each man at his swift oar, and let our ship
sail out on her seaworthy way. Those threats   [250]
our two commanders, sons of Atreus,
keep hurling at us are so serious,
I am afraid of savage death by stoning,
sharing the suffering of the man in there,
struck down with him now in the grip of fate,   300
his own inexorable doom.

TECMESSA

                              No, no.
He is no longer like that. He's grown calm.
Like a sharp south wind that rushes past
without a lightning flash, he's easing off.
Now he's sane again, but in new agonies.
To look at self-inflicted suffering   [260]

17

when no one else played any part in it
brings on great anguish.

CHORUS LEADER
                    If he's no longer mad,
I'm confident that things may be all right.
For when disaster has already passed   310
it doesn't have as much significance.

TECMESSA
But if you had the choice of causing grief
to your own friends while feeling good yourself
or of grieving too, a suffering man
among a common sorrow, which would you choose?

CHORUS LEADER
The double grieving, lady, is far worse.

TECMESSA
So at this moment we, although not sick,
are facing disaster.

CHORUS LEADER
                    What does that mean?
I don't understand what you are saying.   [270]

TECMESSA
That man in there, when he was still so ill,   320
enjoyed himself while savage fantasies
held him in their grip, but we were sane,
and, since he was one of us, we suffered.
But now there is a pause in his disease,
he can recuperate and understand
the full extremity of bitter grief,
yet everything for us remains the same—
our anguish is no milder than before.
This is surely not a single sorrow,
but a double grief?

CHORUS LEADER
                    I think that's true.   330
I fear a blow sent from a god has struck him.
How else could this take place, if his spirit

is no more hopeful now that he's been cured [280]
than when he was sick?

TECMESSA
                    That's how things stand.
    You must see that.

CHORUS LEADER
                    How did his illness start?
    How did this trouble first swoop down on him?
    Since we share your grief, tell us what happened.

TECMESSA
    You are all involved in this, and so you'll hear
    the entire story. At some point in the night,
    when the evening torches had stopped burning,   340
    Ajax took up his two-edged sword, resolved
    to set off on a senseless expedition.
    I challenged him and said, "What are you doing?
    Ajax, why are you going out like this?
    There's been no summons, no messenger,
    nor any trumpet call. All the army   [290]
    is now sleeping." His reply to me was brief,
    that old refrain, "Woman, the finest thing
    that females do is hold their tongues." So I,
    taking my cue from that, did not respond,   350
    and he charged out alone. I cannot say
    what went on out there, but he came back
    and took his chained-up prisoners inside,
    all linked together—bulls and herding dogs
    and captured sheep. He cut the heads off some.
    He twisted back the skulls of other beasts
    and cut their throats or chopped their spines.
    Others, whom he kept tied up, he tortured,
    as if they were human beings, even though   [300]
    it was only beasts he was attacking.   360
    At last, he charged out through the doorway
    and forced out some words of conversation
    with a shadow. Sometimes he'd talk about
    the sons of Atreus, at other times
    about Odysseus, with manic laughter

19

at how by going out he had avenged
all their arrogance in full. After that,
he rushed back in the hut again and there
he gradually regained his sense somehow,
though not without an effort. Once he saw   370
his room filled up with that deluded slaughter,
he struck his head and howled. Then he collapsed,
a ruined man among so many ruins,
carcasses of butchered sheep. He sat there,
fists gripping his hair with nails clenched tight.   [310]
For a long time he remained quite silent.
Then he made some dreadful threats against me
if I would not tell him every detail
of what had taken place. He questioned me—
What on earth had he become involved with?   380
My friends, I was afraid. So I told him
everything that had gone on, all the things
I knew were true. He at once began to groan,
doleful sounds I'd never heard from him before.
He's always claimed that wailing cries like that
were only fit for gloomy men and cowards.   [320]
He used to grieve, but never wail aloud—
just a deep moan, like from a lowing bull.
But now, overwhelmed by his misfortune,
he takes no food, no drink, sprawled in silence   390
where he fell down among dead animals
his own sword killed. It seems clear enough
he will do something bad. The words he speaks
and his laments show that intent somehow.
My friends, you should come in and help him,
if that's possible. That's why I came out here.
For words from friends can cure a man like him.   [330]

CHORUS LEADER
Tecmessa, daughter of Teleutas,
what you've described to us about the man
being driven mad with sorrow—that's dreadful.   400

20

AJAX [crying out from inside the hut]
    Aaaiiii . . . Alas for me!

TECMESSA
    It looks as if his fit could soon be worse.
    Did you not hear that loud cry from Ajax?

AJAX [from inside the hut]
    Aaaiiii! . . . Alas!

CHORUS LEADER
    I think the man is sick or still suffering
    the effects of that disease he had before—
    they're all around him where he sits.

AJAX [from inside the hut]
    My child! My son!

TECMESSA
                    How miserable I feel!   [340]
    Eurysaces, he's calling you. But why?
    What does he have in mind? Where are you?   410
    I'm overwhelmed.

AJAX
                    I call on Teucer!
    Where is Teucer? Will that fighting raid he's on
    keep going forever, with me dying here?[1]

CHORUS LEADER
    I think the man may have his wits again.
    Open the door. Perhaps when he sees me
    he'll quickly feel a sense of self-respect.

TECMESSA [opening the door of the hut]
    There. It's open. Now you can take a look
    at what he's done and see the state he's in.

[AJAX is revealed sitting among the dead animals]

---

[1]Teucer, an important Argive warrior, is Ajax's half-brother.

AJAX

    Ah, my cherished sailors, of all my friends
    the only ones who still observe true loyalty.   420   [350]
    You see how great a wave has just rolled over me,
    a crashing surge lashed on by murderous winds.

CHORUS LEADER *[to Tecmessa]*

    It looks as if what you told us is true—
    his condition clearly shows his madness.

AJAX

    Ah, you race of master mariners,
    who crossed the sea and with your oars sped out
    across the salty ocean, I see in you,
    and in you alone, the one support   [360]
    in my despair. Come, help me kill myself.

CHORUS LEADER

    No more of that! Speak words of hope.   430
    Don't seek to cure one bad thing with another
    or make this mad disaster any worse.

AJAX

    Do you see how this bold and valiant heart,
    this warrior so fearless in those wars
    against his enemies, has turned his hands,
    these awesome hands, against tame animals?
    Ah, the mockery! How I have been abused!

TECMESSA

    I beg you, my lord Ajax, don't say that.

AJAX

    Just go away. Why not turn your feet around
    and wander off somewhere? Aaaaiiii   440   [370]

CHORUS LEADER

    By the gods, concede. Use your common sense.

AJAX

    It's my bad luck I let slip from my grasp
    those criminals deserving punishment.

22

Instead I went at bulls with twisted horns,
fine herds of goats and made their dark blood flow.

CHORUS LEADER
Why lament those deeds which have been done
and cannot be recalled? Such final acts
will never be anything but what they are.

AJAX
O you who keeps prying into everything,
you nasty instrument for every crime,   450   [380]
Odysseus, the filthiest degenerate
in all the army, you must be laughing now,
taking great delight in this.

CHORUS LEADER
                            Divine will
determines if each man laughs and cries.

AJAX
                                        But still
I'd like to face him, though I'm injured. Ahhhh . . . .

CHORUS LEADER
Don't make boasts like that. Do you not see
the catastrophe you face?

AJAX
                        O Zeus,
you ancestral father of my father,
if only I could die after I had killed
that wheedling scoundrel enemy of mine   460   [390]
and those twin-reigning kings.[1]

TECMESSA
                    When you make that prayer,
pray also that I die as well. With you gone,
why should I continue living?

_____

[1]Ajax is son of Telamon, son of Aeacus, son of Zeus.

AJAX

    O darkness, now my daylight,
    O gloom of Erebus, for me
    the brightest light there is,
    take me, take me now
    to live with you.[1] Take me,
    a man no longer worthy to seek help
    from families of gods or men,   470   [400]
    those creatures of a day.
    For Zeus' daughter, brave Athena,
    abuses and destroys me.
    Where can one escape?
    Where could I go and rest?
    If my past fame has been cut down,
    along with these dead beasts beside me,
    then, my friends, if I now seek
    a madman's triumphs, all the army,
    with repeated blows from their own swords   480
    will cut me down as well.

TECMESSA

    How hard it is for me to hear this man,   [410]
    this worthy man, say things he'd never say
    before this happened!

AJAX

    O you paths of the resounding sea!
    You tidal caves and coastal pastures,
    for a long time now, for far too long,
    you have detained me here in Troy.
    But that you will no longer do, no,
    not while I am breathing still.   490
    Let men of sense be sure of that.
    O you streams of the Scamander,
    my neighbour, so friendly to the Argives,   [420]
    you no longer will be seeing Ajax,
    a man whose equal as a warrior—

---

[1]Erebus is part of the gloomy underworld of Hades, the land of the dead.

and I can make this boast—
Troy never saw arriving here from Greece.[1]
But now I lie among this heap, dishonoured.

CHORUS LEADER
I don't have the strength to stop your words
or to let you go on saying such things—   500
you've fallen into such calamity.

AJAX
Alas! Who would ever think my name   [430]
would suit my troubles so poetically?[2]
For I could well cry out two or three times
"Alas for Ajax!"—that shows the magnitude
of the disaster I am going through.
I am the man whose father's excellence
won supreme respect from all the army.
He took the fairest prize and carried home
every glory from the land of Ida.[3]   510
I am his son, who journeyed after him
to this same land of Troy. I'm just as strong,
with the work of my own hands I have attained
achievements just as great, but, as you see,
these Argive insults have quite ruined me.   [440]
And yet I think I can affirm this much—
had Achilles lived and been about to judge
the man who should receive his weapons,
the prize for being the finest man in war,
no soldier would have put his hand on them   520
before I did. But now the sons of Atreus

---

[1]Scamander is the main river flowing near the city of Troy. It is not entirely clear why Ajax calls the river "friendly," since in Homer the god of the river fights against Achilles in order to help the Trojans.

[2]These lines link Ajax's name in Greek (*Aias*) with the Greek verb meaning to cry "Alas" (*aiai*). The similarity is difficult to render precisely in English if one uses the common English name Ajax. The words "Alas for Ajax" have been added in an attempt to make this point somewhat clearer.

[3]Telamon, father of Ajax, had attacked Troy in an earlier expedition with Hercules and had been awarded as a prize Hesione, a princess of Troy (mother of Ajax's half-brother Teucer). Ida is a mountain very close to Troy.

have dealt them to a fellow whose spirit
will stoop to anything, and pushed aside
all those triumphant victories of Ajax.
If with my distorted mind and eyes,
I had not abandoned what I planned,
they would not have had what's mine by right
put to the vote against another man.[1]
But then that goddess with the glaring eyes,   [450]
implacable Athena, Zeus' daughter,   530
threw me over at the very instant
I was steadying my hand against them.
She hurled in me a frenzied sickness,
so blood from grazing beasts would stain my hands,
and those men now can laugh at their escape,
something I did not want. But when a god
commits an injury, the unworthy man
escapes someone more powerful. And now,
what do I do, when I am obviously
hated by the gods, when the Greek army   540
despises me, and everyone in Troy
and on the plain holds me an enemy?
Should I give up my station in the fleet,   [460]
leaving the sons of Atreus alone,
and sail for home across the Aegean Sea?
How could I face my father, Telamon,
when I arrive back there? How could he bear
to see me showing up with nothing,
without the prize for highest excellence
with which he won his own great crown of fame?   550
That's not a thing I could endure to do.
Well, then, should I charge out there on my own
against the Trojan wall, a lone attack,
fight single combats, do something valiant,
and then at last be killed? But that would please

---

[1]Ajax's point here is that if he had not lost his sanity, he would have killed the sons
of Atreus and thus resolved the matter of the voting, which he sees as an injustice,
since the result awarded the weapons to Odysseus.

the sons of Atreus. It must not happen. [470]
I must seek out some act which will reveal
to my old father how, at least by nature,
his own son has not become a coward.
It is dishonourable for any man 560
to crave a lengthy life, once he discovers
the troubles he is in will never change.
What joy is there for him when every day
just follows on another, pulling him away
or pushing him toward death? I would not pay
for any sort of mortal man who's warmed
by futile hopes. A man of noble birth
lives on with honour, or he dies in glory.
Now you've heard everything I have to say. [480]

CHORUS LEADER
No one will ever claim that you, Ajax, 570
have said a word that's illegitimate,
for what you say is born in your own heart.
But you should stop. Get rid of thoughts like these.
Let friends overrule what you're suggesting.

TECMESSA
O my lord Ajax, for human beings
the worst of evils is what they endure
when they're compelled to. Consider me.
I was the daughter of a free-born father,
a wealthy man, if anyone in Phrygia
could be accounted rich. Now I'm a slave, 580
a circumstance the gods somehow made happen—
yes, the gods and especially your strong limbs. [490]
And thus, since I have come into your bed,
I want the best for you. So I beg you,
by Zeus who guards our home, by that bed
where you had sex with me, do not leave me
to the savage insults of your enemies.
Do not abandon me to some strange hand.
For if you die and leave me all alone,
that day you may be sure the Argive men 590
will take me by force, as well as your own son.

27

We will then both lead the lives of slaves.
One of our lords will speak these biting words, [500]
shooting insults at me, "Look here at this,
a bed mate of Ajax, the strongest man
in all our army. What menial chores she does!
How she's changed from such an enviable state!"
Men will talk that way, and then my fate
will wear me down. Those shameful words will stain
you and your family. Respect your father, 600
whom you will leave a miserable old man.
Respect your mother, too, who shares his years.
She keeps begging the gods that you're alive,
that you'll return back home. And, my lord,
have pity for your son. For if you die, [510]
consider how, whenever that day comes,
both he and I will face desolation.
He will lack the nurturing a young lad needs
if you leave and he becomes an orphan,
in the care of people who are not friends 610
or from his family. And I have nothing
I can look to except you. It was you
who killed my homeland for me with your spear.
My mother and my father were destroyed
by a different fate which led them down
to make their home in Hades after death.
What country could I have except with you?
What wealth? My safety, all security,
that rests with you. So remember me as well. [520]
A genuine man should cherish memory, 620
if he gets pleasure still from anything.
Kindness always engenders gratitude.
A man who gives up his good memories
will no longer be a noble, worthy man.

CHORUS LEADER
Ajax, I wish that pity touched your heart,
as it does mine. Then you'd approve her words.

AJAX
So far as I'm concerned, she'll win approval

only if she keeps being obedient
and carries out my orders properly.

TECMESSA
Yes, beloved Ajax, I will obey 630
in everything.

AJAX
Then bring me my son, [530]
so I may see him.

TECMESSA
I sent him away,
out of my care. I was so terrified.

AJAX
Afraid because I was in trouble?
What do you mean?

TECMESSA
Yes, that's it. I feared
that the unlucky boy might bother you
and then somehow get killed.

AJAX
Yes, such a thing
the god who watches me would think fitting.

TECMESSA
At least I took a suitable precaution
to stop that happening.

AJAX
I approve of that. 640
The steps you took were quite correct.

TECMESSA
And so,
as things are now, how can I best serve you?

AJAX
Let me talk to him, see him face to face.

TECMESSA
Yes. He's close by, with servants watching him.

AJAX
Why then this delay? Why is he not here?   [540]

TECMESSA *[calling to the side]*
My son, your father is calling for you.
Whichever of you servants has his hand,
bring the boy out here.

AJAX
       Is he coming, the one you called?
Or did he not hear?

TECMESSA
           The servant's on his way.
He's bringing Eurysaces with him.   650

[Enter the SERVANT leading EURYSACES]

AJAX
Lift him up. Hand the boy to me up here.
He'll have no fear of fresh-spilt blood, no,
not if he's a true-bred son of mine
who shares his father's nature. It is time
he was broken in to that harsh code
his father follows and his nature shaped
to something like my own. O my boy,   [550]
may you have better fortunes than your father,
although remain like him in other ways,
for then you'll never be dishonoured.   660
Now I envy you, and with good reason—
for you have no idea of any troubles.
The sweetest life comes when one senses nothing—
to lack all feeling is a painless evil—
until you learn what joy and sorrow mean.
Once you reach that stage, you must reveal
the kind of man you are, your ancestry,
to those who were your father's enemies.
Meanwhile, you should feed on gentle breezes,
fostering your young life so as to bring   670
your mother joy. I know that no Achaean   [560]
will go at you with insults and contempt,
even when I'm gone. For I am leaving Teucer

30

here with you as guardian of your gates.
He will not falter in his care for you,
although he now is busy far away,
chasing his enemies. But my warriors,
my people of the sea, I charge you now
with the same joyful duty I give Teucer.
Report to him what I have ordered here—   680
he is to take this boy back to my home,
show him to Telamon and Eriboea,
my mother, so he may always comfort them   [570]
in their old age, until the time they reach
the yawning caverns of the gods below.
And none of those who judge our competitions
nor the man who ruined me will offer
my weapons as a prize for the Achaeans.
No, my son, for my sake you will have to take
that broad shield from which you get your name.[1]   690
Hold it up high. Shift it by its well-stitched grip,
my impenetrable seven-layered shield.
My other weapons you will bury with me.
Come, take the boy, and quickly. Close the hut.
And don't keep on weeping here in front.
How these women really love their wailing!   [580]
Quick now, close up the hut. A skilful healer
does not howl incantations when a wound
is crying for the knife.

CHORUS LEADER
                              When I hear
that you're in such a rush, I get afraid.   700
The sharp edge on your tongue brings me no joy.

TECMESSA
O lord Ajax, what are you going to do?

[1] Eurysaces, the name of the child, literally means "broad shield." Ajax's huge shield is described and celebrated in Homer's Iliad.

31

AJAX
Don't keep on asking me! No more questions!
The best thing now is self-restraint.

TECMESSA
                    But I'm desperate!
By the gods, by your own son, I beg you—
do not become a man who now betrays us!

AJAX
You pester me too much. Do you not see
that I no longer owe the gods my service?   [590]

TECMESSA
You must not utter such impieties.

AJAX
Speak to those who listen.

TECMESSA
                    You will not hear me?   710

AJAX
You have already chatted far too much.

TECMESSA
Yes, my lord, because I am so afraid.

AJAX *[to the servants]*
Shut the doors. Do it now!

TECMESSA
                    By all the gods, concede!

AJAX
It looks as though you're thinking like a fool,
if, at this late date, you still believe
that what you teach will shape my character.

[The SERVANTS close the main door of the hut, leaving AJAX still inside. TECMESSA, EURYSACES, and the SERVANTS go into the hut through the side door from which Eurysaces emerged earlier]

CHORUS
O splendid Salamis,

32

you, I know, lie in the sea,
whose waves beat on your happy shores,
a famous place among all men forever.   720
I have been held back a long time here   [600]
in misery, for countless months
still camped out in the fields of Ida,
consumed by time and my anxiety,
expecting to complete my journey
to implacably destructive Hades.

And now my troubles multiply,
a situation hard to remedy,
for I must wrestle now with Ajax,   [610]
share my life with that insanity   730
sent from the gods. Alas for me!
Once, long ago, you sent him out
filled with the frenzied power of war.
But now his spirit feeds in isolation,
and his friends acquire from him
a heavy sorrow. His earlier deeds,
those acts of highest excellence,
have fallen, fallen where he has no friends,
among the wretched hostile sons of Atreus.   [620]

The years have changed his mother's hair to white,   740
and given her old age for company.
When she learns of his disease,
that maddening infection of his mind,
she'll start to wail forth her laments.
She will not chant out melodies
sung by the plaintive nightingale.
No. In her mood of desolation   [630]
the sharp-toned music of her grief
will scream abroad her anguish.
Her beating hands will thud down on her breasts,   750
and she'll keep tearing out her old gray hair.

A man brain sick with mad delusions
is better off concealed in Hades,
a man who by his ancestry
is ranked the best of the Achaeans,

33

who have endured so much. But now,
no longer following his inbred character,
he wanders far beyond himself.   [640]
O you unhappy father Telamon,
you have yet to hear the heavy curse   760
laid on your son, a curse which up to now
has never played a part in any life
nurtured by the sons of Aeacus.

*[Enter AJAX through the main doors of the hut, carrying a sword.
TECMESSA enters after him.]*

AJAX
The long succession of the countless years
reveals what's hidden, then hides it once again,
and there is nothing we should not anticipate.
The solemn oath and the most stubborn heart
are overcome. In this way, even I,   [650]
who used to be so marvellously strong,
like tempered iron, felt my sharp edge dissolve 770
at what this woman said. I now feel pity
leaving her a widow and my son an orphan
among my enemies. And so I'll go
to the bathing waters by the sea shore
and wash off my defilement. I will deflect
the weighty anger of the goddess there.
When I leave, I'll find some isolated place
and then inter my sword, of all my weapons
the one I most despise. I'll dig the earth
where no one else will see. Then let Night   780
and Hades keep it there below the ground.   [660]
For ever since I've held it in my grip,
this gift from Hector, my greatest enemy,
I've won no prizes from the Argives.[1]
That old human saying is true: gifts men get

[1]Homer recounts in the *Iliad* how Ajax received a sword from Hector, the great
Trojan warrior-prince, in a mutual exchange of gifts, when their single combat was
halted by both armies.

from enemies—they are no gifts at all
and bring them no advantages. And so,
from this day forward I shall understand
how to revere the gods. And I will learn
how to respect the sons of Atreus.   790
They are our rulers, so we must obey.
Why not? Things of the greatest power and awe
give way to privileged authorities.   [670]
Snow-footed Winter yields to fruitful Summer,
and Night's dark vault withdraws the moment Day
with her white-footed horses fires up the sky;
the blasts of fearful Winds at last bring rest
which calms the groaning seas. All-powerful Sleep
lets go the one he holds tied up in chains;
his grasp does not go on forever. As for us,   800
how can we mortals not learn self-control?
I, at least, am only now discovering
that we should hate our enemies as much
as suits a man who will become a friend.   [680]
And when I help a friend, then I will give
only what is due a man who'll not remain
a friend forever. For common mortals
see that the shelter comradeship affords
is treacherous. Thus, my situation
will turn out for the best. And so, woman,   810
go inside now. Keep praying to the gods
my heart's desires will reach fulfillment
and be carried out to their conclusion.

*[TECMESSA return into the hut through the side door. AJAX turns
to address the CHORUS]*

AJAX

My comrades, you, too, honour this request.
Tell Teucer, when he comes, to care for me
and also to protect your interests.
I am now going where I have to go.   [690]
As for you, carry out what I have said,
and very soon, perhaps, you will find out
that, though I'm suffering now, I am at peace.   820

35

[AJAX leaves, heading for the sea shore.]

CHORUS
    I feel a sudden thrill of passionate delight,
    which makes me soar aloft with happiness
        and cry with joy to Pan—
          O Pan, Pan—
      appear to us, sea rover—
    come down from your stony ridge
    on snow-beat Mount Cyllene,
    you dancing master of the gods—
        come, O king,
    begin your self-taught dancing steps   830
      from Mysia and Cnossos,   [700]
    for what I want now is to dance.
    And may Apollo, lord of Delos,
      race across the Icarian Sea
    and manifest himself to me,
    show his benevolence in everything.

    From our eyes Ares has removed
      those terrifying agonies.
        What joy! O joy!
      For now, O Zeus, now   840
    the dazzling light of brighter days
    can come to our swift ships
    which speed across the seas,   [710]
    for Ajax is free of pain once more
    and, in a transformed state of mind,
    has carried out appropriate sacrifice
    to all the gods in full, showing them
    due reverence and strictly following
      our most important laws.
The power of time extinguishes all things,   850
    so I can't say that anything
    lies beyond all expectation—
since, in contrast to what we were waiting for,
    now Ajax's mind has changed again
    away from actions done in anger
    and his great fight with Atreus' sons.

[*Enter the MESSENGER*]

MESSENGER
  Friends, the first thing I have to report is this—
  Teucer has just come from the Mysian heights.   [720]
  He's now in the middle of our line of ships,
  in the generals' camp. All the Argives   860
  are shouting insults at him, all at once.
  They saw him coming and, as he approached,
  surrounded him, hurling accusations
  from all directions—everyone joined in—
  calling him the brother of that maniac
  who had conspired against the army
  and saying he could not escape his death—
  their stones would cut him down completely.
  Things reached the point where men had pulled their swords
  out of their scabbards and held them fully drawn.   870
  Then, as the fight was getting out of hand,
  some elders intervened. Their words stopped it.
  But where can I find Ajax to tell him this?
  I must provide our king a full report.

CHORUS LEADER
  He's not inside. He has just gone away,
  with new intentions yoked to his changed mood.

MESSENGER
  O no! No! Then the man who sent me here
  did so too late, or I have been too slow.

CHORUS LEADER
  What's so urgent? What's been overlooked?   [740]

MESSENGER
  Teucer said that Ajax had to stay inside   880
  and not leave his hut until he gets here.

CHORUS LEADER
  Well, as I told you, Ajax has gone off.
  He intends to follow now what's best for him,
  to cleanse away his anger at the gods.

37

MESSENGER

    Your words reveal your complete foolishness,
    if what Calchas prophesies has any merit.[1]

CHORUS LEADER

    What do you mean? What information
    do you have about what's happening here?

MESSENGER

    Well I was there, so I know this much—
    I witnessed it. Calchas left the leaders   890
    sitting in their royal council circle,
    moving off from the sons of Atreus.   [750]
    In a friendly gesture he placed his right hand
    in Teucer's palm. Then he spoke to him,
    giving him strict orders to use every means
    to keep Ajax in his hut while this day lasts
    and to prevent him moving anywhere
    if he ever wished to see him still alive.
    For divine Athena's rage would whip Ajax
    only for that day. That's what Calchas said.   900
    Then the prophet added, "Those living things
    which become too large and thus unwieldy
    fall into harsh disasters from the gods—
    the sort of man who, born from human stock,   [760]
    forgets and thinks beyond his mortal state.
    Take Ajax. As soon as he set out from home,
    he revealed his folly, though his father
    had passed on good advice. For Telamon
    commanded him, 'My son, with that spear of yours
    you must seek victory, but always fight   910
    with some god at your side.' But then Ajax,
    in a lofty boast, thoughtlessly replied,
    'Father, with god's help even a worthless man
    can be victorious. But I believe
    I'll win glory on my own without them.'
    Such was his arrogance. Another time,   [770]

---

[1]Calchas is the most important prophet and soothsayer with the Argive army.

with divine Athena, as she was rousing him
and telling him to turn his deadly hands
against the enemy, he answered her
with a fearful and sacrilegious speech,   920
'Lady, stand there with the other Argives.
The fight will never break the line through Ajax.'
It was with words like these that he provoked
the unremitting anger of the goddess,
because he does not think as humans should.
But if he remains alive all day today,
with god's help we might be his saviours."
That's what Calchas said. From where he sat   [780]
Teucer sent me off at once with orders
which you were meant to follow. If we fail,   930
Ajax is done for—that is, if Calchas
has any skill in prophecy.

CHORUS LEADER [calling into the side door of the hut]
                         Tecmessa,
unfortunate lady born for sorrow,
come out and see this man. Hear his news.
The razor's slicing closer. I feel its pain.

[Enter TECMESSA through the side door of the hut]

TECMESSA
Why are you making me come out once more
and leave the chair where I was getting
some relief from these unending troubles?

CHORUS LEADER
Listen to this man—he's come with news
about what is happening with Ajax,   940   [790]
and it's disturbing.

TECMESSA
                         O no! You there,
tell me what you have to say. Does this mean
we're finished?

MESSENGER
                         I have no idea

39

how things stand with you. As for Ajax,
if he is not inside, then I've lost hope.

TECMESSA
He's gone away. So I'm in agony
about just what you mean.

MESSENGER
                    Teucer gave orders
that you keep Ajax safely in his hut
and do not let him leave all by himself.

TECMESSA
But where is Teucer? Why did he say that?   950

MESSENGER
He has only just returned. He suspects
if Ajax goes somewhere he'll be destroyed.

TECMESSA
That's horrible! What man told him this?   [800]

MESSENGER
Thestor's son, the prophet, whose words proclaimed
this very day would bring life or death for Ajax.

TECMESSA
O my friends, protect me from this destiny!
Some of you, get Teucer here more quickly,
while others go off to the western cove
and to the east, as well, to investigate—
find out where Ajax went, when he set off   960
on that ill-fated path. For now I know
I have, in fact, been totally deceived,
and Ajax has finally cast away
all that affection he once had for me.
Alas, my son, what am I going to do?
I can't stay idle. So I'll go out there,   [810]
as far as I have strength to go. Let's leave—
and hurry! This is no time to sit around,
if we want to save a man who's eager
for destruction.

40

CHORUS LEADER

              I'm prepared to help,   970
not just with words, as I will demonstrate.
If we move fast, we can do this quickly.

[They all exit in various directions, leaving the stage empty. The scene now changes to a deserted part of the seashore. AJAX enters, carrying his sword, which he sets upright in the sand, with the blade sticking upward.]

AJAX

The sacrificial killer is in place,
so it will now cut most effectively.
If a man had time, he might reflect on this.
It is a gift from Hector, a warrior
who was a friend most hateful to me,
the one I looked on as my greatest foe.[1]
Then, this sword is firmly set in Trojan soil,
land of my enemy, freshly whetted   980
on the iron-eating sharpening stone.   [820]
And I have fixed it in the ground with care,
so it will kill me quickly and be kind.
Thus, we are well prepared. So, O Zeus,
in this situation, be the first to help,
as is appropriate. I'm not asking you
to give me a grand prize, but for my sake
send a messenger to carry this bad news
to Teucer, so he may be the first
to raise me, once I've fallen on the sword   990
and covered it with fresh-spilt blood. Don't let
the first to spot me be some enemy,
who'll throw me out, exposed as carrion food   [830]
for dogs and birds. I appeal to you, O Zeus.
Grant me this much. I also call on Hermes,
guide to the world below, to let me sleep

---

[1]In the *Iliad*, after their single combat had been halted, Hector and Ajax ceremoniously pledged friendship in a mutual exchange of gifts. Yet Hector, as leader of the Trojans and their greatest warrior, was also Ajax's most important enemy.

without convulsions, when by one quick leap
I break my bones apart on this sharp blade.
And I summon those immortal maidens
to my aid, those who always see all things   1000
of human suffering, the dread, far-striding Furies,
to witness how, in my wretchedness,
the sons of Atreus worked my destruction.[1]
May they seize on them and destroy them, too,
with deaths as vile as their disgusting selves.   [840]
Just as they see me killed by my own hand,
so let them perish, killed by their own kindred,
the children they love most. Come, you Furies,
you swift punishers, devour the army,
all of them, sparing no one. And you, Helios,   1010
whose chariot wheels climb that steep path to heaven,
when you look down over my father's land,
pull back those reins of yours, which flash with gold,
then tell the story of my miseries,
my destiny, to my old father
and to the unhappy one who nursed me.[2]
That poor lady, when she hears this news,   [850]
will, I think, sing out a huge lamenting dirge
throughout the city. But for me to weep
is useless. It's time to start the final act.   1020
O Death, Death, come now and watch in person.
Yet I'll be seeing you on the other side,
and there we can converse. And so to you,
the radiant light of this bright shining day,
I make my final call, and to the Sun—
I'll never see that chariot any more.
O light, O sacred land of Salamis,
my home, my father's sturdy hearth,   [860]
and glorious Athens, whose race was bred
related to my own—and you rivers,   1030
you streams, you plains of Troy, I call on you.

[1]The Furies are the goddesses of blood revenge.

[2]Helios is the god of the sun. His chariot carries the sun through its daily journey.

Farewell, you who have nurtured me—to you
Ajax now speaks his final words. The rest
I'll say to those below in Hades.

[Ajax falls on his sword. Enter the CHORUS in two groups from two different directions. Each has a separate leader. They do not see Ajax's body until Tecmessa finds it.] [1]

CHORAL GROUP 1
We work and work,
and that brings on more work.
Where have I not walked? Where?
No place where I have searched
has revealed to me where Ajax is.
What's that? Listen! I heard a noise.   1040   [870]

CHORAL GROUP 2 LEADER
It's us—the crew that shares the ships with you.

CHORAL GROUP 1 LEADER
What can you report?

CHORAL GROUP 2 LEADER
                We've searched everywhere
on the west side of the ships.

CHORAL GROUP 1 LEADER
Did you come up with anything?

CHORAL GROUP 2 LEADER
Just lots of work. There's nothing there to see.

CHORAL GROUP 1 LEADER
Well, we haven't seen him either—
not on the path facing the rising sun.

CHORUS
Who then can lead me on,

---

[1] The suicide of Ajax provides a very rare example in Greek tragedy of a killing performed on stage. It is not clear, however, if it was done in full view of the audience or whether it was concealed somehow by a stage prop (like a bush). Ajax's body is not plainly visible to anyone who wanders past, since it remains hidden from the Chorus for some time.

what toiling sons of the sea, [880]
sleepless in their shacks? 1050
What nymph on high Olympus
or from the streams that flow
into the Bosphorus
could say if she has seen somewhere
fierce-hearted Ajax wandering around?
It is not fair that after a long search
and so much effort I can't find
the proper path to him. I cannot see
where that elusive man might be. [890]

[Enter TECMESSA behind the Chorus. As she moves on, she trips on the corpse of Ajax]

TECMESSA
Ahhh . . . .

CHORUS LEADER
           Who cried out? It sounded close, 1060
from that group of trees.

TECMESSA
          O how horrible . . . .

CHORUS LEADER
I see her, the unfortunate young bride,
Tecmessa, a prize won with his spear—
she's lying there, prostrate with grief, in pain . . .

TECMESSA
I'm lost . . . destroyed . . . my life is over.
O my friends. . . .

CHORUS LEADER
     What's happened?

TECMESSA
               It's our Ajax—
he's lying here . . . he's just been murdered,
his body's wrapped around a buried sword.

CHORUS LEADER
O no! Our dreams of getting home are gone. [900]

44

Alas, my king, you have destroyed me, too,   1070
the one who sailed across the seas with you . . . .
you poor, unhappy man . . . heart-sick lady . . .

TECMESSA

With Ajax dead like this, we have good cause
to wail out our grief.

CHORUS LEADER

                              Who did this?
With whose help could ill-fated Ajax
have gone through with this?

TECMESSA

                              He did it by himself.
That's clear. This sword fixed upright in the ground
indicates he fell down on top of it.

CHORUS LEADER

Alas, for my own foolishness!
You bled to death alone, with no friends there   1080   [910]
to keep an eye on you. I was so stupid,
so blind to everything. I took no care.
And now, now where does stubborn Ajax lie,
a man whose very name suggests misfortune.[1]

TECMESSA

He's not a spectacle to gaze upon!
With this cloak I will cover him completely,
tuck it all around him—for nobody,
at least no one who was a friend of his,
could bear to see him, as he spurts blood
up his nostrils and from that dark red wound,   1090
his self-inflicted slaughter. Alas!
What shall I do? What friend of yours   [920]
will lift you up for burial? Where's Teucer?
How I wish that he would come right now,
when we need him—if he ever comes

---

[1]Ajax's name, as mentioned above, is very similar to the Greek verb *aiai*, "to cry alas!"

to care for the body of his brother.
O ill-fated Ajax, how could a man like you
end up like this? Even your enemies
must find you worthy of a funeral song.

CHORUS
O you unhappy man, how you were doomed,   1100
with that unbending heart of yours,
fated to live out an evil destiny
of endless suffering.
I know you groaned such hostile words   [930]
against the sons of Atreus
all night long and in the morning light,
the fatal passion of a stubborn heart.
It's obvious that when those weapons
were made the prizes in the competition
for the finest of our battle warriors,   1110
that was a potent source of trouble.

TECMESSA
Alas! Alas for me!

CHORUS LEADER
                Your heart, I know,
is truly filled with grief.

TECMESSA
                Such misery for me!

CHORUS LEADER
It's no surprise to me, my lady,   [940]
you wail and wail again, for you've just lost
a man you loved so much.

TECMESSA
                You only guess
how it must feel, but I experience it,
and to the limit.

CHORUS LEADER
                That's true enough.

46

TECMESSA

Alas, my son, what kind of slavery
will yoke us now as we move on from here,   1120
what sort of taskmasters stand over us?

CHORUS LEADER

Ah, now you've given voice to your concerns
about unspeakable actions by those men,
the two unfeeling sons of Atreus,
in this our present grief. May god restrain them!

TECMESSA

But these events would not have taken place   [950]
without the gods' consent.

CHORUS LEADER

                    Yes—they have set
a burden too heavy for us to bear.

TECMESSA

It's Athena, Zeus' savage daughter.
What miseries that goddess has produced,   1130
and for Odysseus' sake.

CHORUS LEADER

                    I'm sure that man,
who has endured so much, in his black heart
exults and laughs with lofty arrogance
at these insane disasters. Such mockery!
Such a disgrace! And when they hear of this,
those two royal sons of Atreus
will join his merriment.   [960]

TECMESSA

                    Then let them laugh!
Let them get their joy from this man's agony.
Although they did not sense their need of him
while he was living, perhaps they'll mourn his death   1140
when they need him in war. Men with brutal minds
have no idea what fine things they possess
until they throw them out. Ajax's death—
to me so bitter and to them so sweet—

47

at least has brought him joy, for he has got
what he desired, the death he yearned for.
So why should these men make fun of him?
His death is the gods' concern, not theirs. No! [970]
So let Odysseus vaunt his empty jests.
For them Ajax is dead—for me he's gone, 1150
abandoning me to grief and mourning.

TEUCER [heard offstage]
                    No, no . . . No!

CHORUS LEADER
    Be quiet. I think I hear Teucer's voice.
    His shouts send out a tone which penetrates
    the heart of this disaster.

[Enter TEUCER]

TEUCER [moving up to Ajax's body]
                    O dearest Ajax,
    my bright source of joy, my brother,
    what's happened to you. Is the rumour true?

CHORUS LEADER
    He's dead, Teucer. That's the truth.

TEUCER
    Alas! Then I bear a heavy destiny! [980]

CHORUS LEADER
    Given how things stand . . . .

TEUCER
                    This is too sad.

CHORUS LEADER
    . . . you have good cause to grieve.

TEUCER
                    This act of his, 1160
    so rash and passionate . . . .

CHORUS LEADER
                    Yes, Teucer,
    passion in excess.

48

TEUCER

                This is disastrous.
What about his son? Where on Trojan soil
can I find him?

CHORUS LEADER

          He's in the hut—all by himself.

TEUCER [To Tecmessa]

You—bring him here as soon as possible,
in case he gets snatched by an enemy,
the way a hunter grabs a lion cub
and leaves its mother childless. Go quickly!
We need your help. For it's a fact all men
love to laugh in triumph above the dead,   1170
when they're stretched out before them.

[Exit TECMESSA]

CHORUS LEADER

               Teucer,
when Ajax was alive, he said that you   [990]
should look after his son, as you're now doing.

TEUCER

O this is surely the most painful sight
of anything my eyes have ever seen.
And, of all the roads I've travelled, the worst,
the one most deeply painful to my heart,
is that pathway I've just walked along,
while trying to track you down, dearest Ajax,
once I'd learned your fate. There was some gossip,   1180
some tale to do with you. It spread quickly,
as if sent by a god, to all the Argives.
It said that you had wandered off and died.
I heard the details far away from here
and there I groaned with sorrow. Now I'm here,
I see it for myself. It breaks my heart.   [1000]
It's dreadful. Come, take off this covering,
so I get a full view of this horror.

[Attendants remove the cloak covering Ajax's body]

49

O that face—it's so painful to see now,
so full of bitter daring. How many sorrows   1190
you have sown for me by this destruction!
Where can I go? What sort of people
will take me in, when I was no use to you
in times of trouble? No doubt Telamon,
who fathered you and me, will welcome me,
perhaps with smiles and words of kindness,
when I reach home without you. Of course he will!   [1010]
For he's the kind of man who never smiles,
not cheerfully, even when things go well.
A man like that—what will he not say?   1200
What sort of insult will he not hurl at me—
a bastard spawned by some battle-prize of his,
who, because of his unmanly cowardice,
betrayed you, dearest Ajax, or by treachery
tried to seize your power and your home,
once you were dead. That's what Telamon will say.
He's a bad-tempered man, and his old age
has made him harsh—his anger likes to argue
over nothing. He'll end up banishing me,
throw me from the land. What he'll say of me   1210
will make me seem a slave instead of free.   [1020]
That's what will happen if I go back home.
Here in Troy I have many enemies,
and few ways of getting help. All this
has happened to me because you've been killed.
It's a disaster. What am I to do?
How do I raise you up, you sad corpse,
from the sharp bite of this glittering sword,
your murderer, on which you breathed your last?
You've come to sense how, in good time, Hector,   1220
though dead, was going to slaughter you. Look here,
by the gods—see the fate of these two men.
First, Hector was lashed tight to that chariot rail   [1030]
with the very belt Ajax had given him,
and underwent continual mutilation
until he gasped his life away. Then Ajax
took Hector's gift in hand and used it

50

to kill himself in that death-dealing fall.[1]
Surely a vengeful Fury forged this blade,
and that harsh craftsman Hades made that belt?   1230
For my part, I would assert that gods
have plotted these events—they always do
in everything that mortal men go through.
If someone finds this view objectionable,
let him love his own beliefs, as I do mine.

CHORUS LEADER
Don't stay too long. You need to think   [1040]
how we can bury Ajax. And what to say.
It's urgent. For someone coming here,
a man who is our enemy. It could be
he comes to mock at our misfortunes, a man   1240
who thrives on harm.

TEUCER
                    Who is it—the man you see?
What member of the army?

CHORUS LEADER
                                        It's Menelaus,
the one for whom we launched this expedition.

TEUCER
I see him. He's not hard to recognize
when he's so close.

[Enter MENELAUS, with a small escort of soldiers]

MENELAUS
                    You there—I order you
not to take up that corpse for burial.
Leave it where it is.

---

[1]When Ajax and Hector fought in single combat in the *Iliad*, as mentioned earlier, the fight was stopped and the two warriors exchanged gifts. Ajax gave Hector a fine belt, and Hector presented a sword to Ajax. When Achilles later fought and defeated Hector, he tied Hector's body to his chariot and desecrated the body by dragging it around in the dirt for days. However, in Homer's account, Hector is clearly dead before this mutilation of his corpse starts.

TEUCER

        Why waste your words
with such an order?

MENELAUS

            I think it's fitting,   [1050]
as does the commander of our army.

TEUCER

Then would it bother you to tell me why   1250
you issue this command?

MENELAUS

               The reason's this:
we hoped that we were leading Ajax here,
away from home, so he'd be our ally,
someone friendly to the Argives, but instead,
when we saw him more closely, we found out
he was more hostile than the Phrygians.[1]
He planned to destroy our entire army
and set off at night to take us with his spear.
If some god had not frustrated his attempt,
we would have met the same fate he did—   1260
we'd be dead and lying there, struck down
by shameful fate, and he'd be still alive.   [1060]
But now, it's clear a god changed these events,
and so the violence in his heart fell elsewhere,
on sheep and cattle. And that's the reason
there's no one powerful enough right now
to take his corpse and set it in a grave.
Instead it will be tossed away somewhere
on the yellow sand, food for shore birds.
Remember that. Curb the anger in your heart.   1270
If we could not control him when he lived,
at least he will obey us now he's dead.
Even if you don't agree, our forceful hands
will take charge of him. When he was alive,

---

[1] Phrygia was an extensive area to the east of Troy (now modern Turkey). Here the word means Trojans generally.

Ajax never listened to a word I said.   [1070]
And it's a fact that when a common man
thinks it's appropriate to disobey
those in command, he truly demonstrates
his worthless character. Within the city
the laws could never foster benefits   1280
if there was no established place for fear.
Nor can one lead the troops with wise restraint
where there is neither fear or reverence
to act in their defence. So any man,
no matter how powerful his body grows,
must realize he'll fall, even when
the harm to him seems trivial. A man
who has in him a sense of fear and shame
is quite secure—you can be sure of that—   [1080]
but where there's room for hostile arrogance   1290
and men do what they want, consider how
a state like that, though it has raced ahead
with favouring winds, will, in the course of time,
sink in the ocean depths eventually.
And so for me let fear be set in place
where it's appropriate. Let's not believe
we can just do whatever we desire
and not pay the painful consequence.
These matters fluctuate—Ajax was once
a man of fiery insolence, but now   1300
it's time for me to manifest my power.
And thus I warn you not to bury him.   [1090]
If you do, you just might fall yourself
into your grave.

CHORUS LEADER
                              Menelaus,
after setting out such well-thought precepts,
do not become too arrogant yourself
in dealing with the dead.

TEUCER
                              Fellow soldiers,
never again will I be much surprised

53

if someone born a nobody goes wrong,
since those apparently of noble birth   1310
can make so many errors when they speak.
Come, tell me once more from the beginning—
do you really think it was you personally
who led Ajax here an Argive ally?
Did he not sail to Troy all on his own,
under his own command? In what respect
are you this man's superior? On what ground   [1100]
do you have any right to rule those men
whom he led here from home? You came to Troy
as king of Sparta. You do not govern us.   1320
Under no circumstance did some right to rule
or give him orders lie within your power,
just as he possessed no right to order you.
You sailed here a subordinate to others,
not as commander of the entire force
who could at any time tell Ajax what to do.
Go, be king of those you rule by right—
use those proud words of yours to punish them.
But I will set this body in a grave,
as justice says I should, even though you   1330
or any other general forbids it.
I am not afraid of your pronouncements.
Ajax did not join the expedition
because that woman was a wife of yours,
as did those toiling Spartan drudges—no—
but because he'd sworn an oath to do it.[1]
You were no part of it. He never valued
men worth nothing. And so when you return,
come back here and bring more heralds with you,
as well as the commander. Your vain chat   1340
is not something that really bothers me,
not while you stay the kind of man you are.

---

[1]Teucer is perhaps splitting hairs here. Ajax was one of the suitors seeking to marry
Helen, and, along with all the others, he swore to assist the man Helen chose to
marry if called upon. That oath was not directed at Menelaus specifically, but once
he became Helen's husband, it applied to him.

CHORUS LEADER
    When things go badly, I don't like to hear
    a tone like that. Even when it's justified,
    harsh language stings.

MENELAUS
                    This mere archer   [1120]
    seems to entertain some big ideas.[1]

TEUCER
                        Indeed I do.
    My skill is not something to underrate.

MENELAUS
    My, my—if only you possessed a shield,
    how grand your boasts would be.

TEUCER
                    Even with no shield,
    I'd get the better of you fully armed.   1350

MENELAUS
    That tongue of yours, how it likes to feed
    the savage spirit inside!

TEUCER
                    When a man is right,
    he's entitled to make impressive claims.

MENELAUS
    Do you mean to tell me it is just
    for someone to be treated generously
    when he's killed me?

TEUCER
                Killed you? Your words sound odd,
    if, after being killed, you are now alive.

---

[1]Teucer was one of the finest archers in the Argive forces. Archers were, however, held in some contempt because, unlike spearman, they did not fight hand to hand in the front ranks but from a distance, often protected by a spearman.

MENELAUS

Some god saved me. As far as Ajax knows,
I'm dead and gone.

TEUCER

Since the gods rescued you,
you should not dishonour them.

MENELAUS

You mean 1360
I could be violating sacred laws? [1130]

TEUCER

Yes, if you personally intervened
to prevent the burial of the dead.

MENELAUS

That's not so with a personal enemy.
To bury him would not be right.

TEUCER

What's that?
Did Ajax ever march ahead in battle
as your enemy?

MENELAUS

He hated me,
and I hated him. But you knew that.

TEUCER

Yes, he did, because you were found out—
you tampered with the vote which robbed him. 1370

MENELAUS

The judges beat him in that competition,
not me.

TEUCER

With your deceitful secrecy
you can conceal so many crimes.

MENELAUS

Words like that
could well prove painful to someone I know.

TEUCER
    Well, I don't think they will bring more pain
    than we'll inflict.

MENELAUS
                    Once and for all, then,   [1140]
    I tell you this: that man will not be buried.

TEUCER
    Then hear my answer: Ajax's corpse
    will have a burial.

MENELAUS
                I have already seen a man
    with a bold tongue urging sailors on   1380
    to launch a voyage during winter storms.
    But you could hear no sound from him at all
    once the storm got nasty. He hid himself
    under a cloak and then let the sailors
    step on him at will. You're just like him,
    you and your braggart mouth—a mighty squall,
    even from a tiny cloud, in no time
    will snuff out your constant shouting.

TEUCER
    And I have seen a man stuffed with stupidity,   [1150]
    whose pride delighted in his neighbours' grief.   1390
    Then someone like me, with my temperament,
    faced up to him and said something like this,
    "Hey, you there, don't harm the dead. If you do,
    you can be sure you'll find yourself in trouble."
    So he warned the paltry fellow face to face.
    I see him now, and it appears to me
    he is none other than yourself. I trust
    I haven't talked too much in riddles?

MENELAUS
    I'm leaving. It would be a great disgrace
    if men found out I've started arguing   1400   [1160]
    when I could use my power.

57

TEUCER

Be off with you!
It would be a great disgrace to me
to listen to such silly chattering
from some fool.

[MENELAUS and his escort leave the way they came]

CHORUS LEADER

We're going to see
a major altercation from this argument.
As quickly as you can, Teucer, you should make
a hollow grave for Ajax, where he'll rest
in a dark tomb, and people for all time
will keep him in their memory.

[Enter TECMESSA and EURYSACES]

TEUCER

Ah, just in time—
his woman and his son have now arrived   1410   [1170]
to perform a funeral for this sad corpse.
Come, lad, move over here. Stand there by him.
Set your hand in supplication on him,
on your father, from whom you were born.
Kneel down in prayer—hold firmly in your hand
locks of hair from me, from her, from you—
the three of us. These give the suppliant strength.[1]
If any member of the army tries
to remove you from this corpse by force,
then may that wicked man become an exile,   1420
tossed out from his own land in misery,
and remain unburied, his roots severed
from his whole race, just as I cut this hair.
Take this, my boy, and guard it. And don't let   [1180]
any man push you away. Stay kneeling here,
and hang on tight. You sailors over there,

---

[1]Offering locks of hair at the tomb of the departed was an important part of the funeral ritual, giving power to the prayers of those mourning the dead.

don't stand around the place like women.
You're men. Stand on guard here, and protect him,
till I get back, once I've set up the grave.
I don't care who has forbidden it.   1430

[Exit TEUCER]

CHORUS
When will our last year here arrive?
When will the number of those wandering years
come to an end—and my interminable fate
to go on carrying this toiling spear
across the wide expanse of Troy,   [1190]
a sorrow and a shame for Greeks?

How I wish that man had been swept off
high into the great sky or into Hades,
the home that all men share,
before he'd introduced the Greeks   1440
to that war mood which sucks up everyone,
those weapons of the god of war,
which every man detests.
O those toils which just produce more toil!
That man has wiped out our humanity.

He gave me as my portion no delight
in garlands or full cups of wine,   [1200]
no sweet tunes from flutes around me,
that ill-fated wretch, or in the night
the joys of sleep. And as for love—alas!—   1450
he has denied me love. I lie here
forgotten, my hair always drenched
from thickly falling dew, ah yes,
my memories from desolate Troy.   [1210]

Bold Ajax used to be my rampart once,
my constant wall against night fears
and flying weapons aimed at me.
But he has now become a sacrifice
to some malevolent deity.
What pleasure, then, what joy   1460
now lies in store for me?

59

O how I wish I were back there,
where the wooded wave-washed headland
juts out, our guard against the open sea,
below the high flat rock of Sunium,   [1220]
and we could then greet sacred Athens.[1]

[Enter TEUCER, in a hurry]

TEUCER
I've just seen commander Agamemnon.
He coming here, and quickly. So I ran back.
He's clearly going to give his blundering mouth
some exercise.

[Enter AGAMEMNON with an armed escort]

AGAMEMNON
                              You there—I've been told   1470
you've dared to mouth foul threats against us
with impunity. I'm talking about you,
the son of a mere slave, a battle trophy.
If some well-bred lady were your mother,
no doubt your boasts would soar high in the sky,   [1230]
and you would strut around on tip toe.
You are a nobody, and here you act
the champion for this nonentity.
In all seriousness you made the claim
we voyaged here with no authority,   1480
as commanders of the troops or of the fleet,
to give orders to Achaeans or to you,
since Ajax sailed under his own command.
Is it not shameful that I have to hear
such monstrous insults from the mouths of slaves?
This man you shout about with so much pride,
what sort of man was he? Where did he go
or stand and fight, where I was not there, too?
Do the Achaeans have no man but him?

---

[1]Sunium is an important cape near Athens, separating the open sea from the safer
waters of the gulf.

It seems it was a painful thing we did   1490
when we announced to all Achaeans
that competition for Achilles' weapons,   [1240]
if in every quarter we appear corrupt,
thanks to Teucer, and if you people here
never will be satisfied, not even
after you have been put down, and yield
to what most of the judges thought was fair.
Instead you will no doubt keep hurling at us
these constant gibes, or from the rearmost ranks
treacherously lash out at us. In places   1500
where such conditions hold you'll never find
a settled order based on rule of law,
not if we discard the men who justly win
and put in front the ones who lag behind.
No We must prevent such tendencies.   [1250]
It's not the big, broad-shouldered warriors
who make the most reliable allies—
it's men who think—they win out every time.
One guides a broad-backed ox straight down the path
with only a small whip. And I can see   1510
you'll soon receive some of that medicine,
unless you get yourself some common sense.
That man is no longer living—by this time
he has become a shade, and here you are
rashly insulting us, letting your mouth
run on and on. You should control yourself.
Do you not realize who you are by birth?
Why not let another man step forward,   [1260]
someone free born, to state your case to us
instead of you? For when you're speaking,   1520
I'm not prepared to listen any more.
To me your barbarian way of speaking
is quite impossible to understand.[1]

---

[1]The term "barbarian" is, one assumes a reference to Teucer's mother, who was a
Phrygian, and therefore an insult to Teucer.

CHORUS LEADER
I wish you two were sensible enough
to show some self-restraint. Nothing I say
would be more useful to the both of you.

TEUCER [addressing the corpse of Ajax]
Well now, how quickly among mortal men
grateful thoughts about the dead are gone
and turn into betrayal. This man here
can't even manage a few words, Ajax,   1530
to celebrate your memory, and yet
you often risked your life protecting him,
hefting that spear of yours in battle.   [1270]
But now, as you can see, all those great deeds
are dead and gone, all thrown aside.

[Teucer turns to address Agamemnon]

                              And you,
you talk a lot of a utter foolishness.
Have you no longer any memory
of the time when you were all bunched up
inside the rampart, almost done for
in that spear fight—then Ajax showed up,   1540
all on his own, and kept protecting you,
with flames already blazing on your ships,
spreading across the decks right at the stern,
and Hector leaping high across the ditch,
heading for our fleet? Who held him back?   [1280]
Was Ajax not the one who managed that,
the man you claim never went any place
where you did not go, too? Do you concede
his actions then, as far as you're concerned,
set a high standard? And then another time,   1550
when he faced up to Hector by himself
in single combat. No one ordered him.
He was picked out by lot, and his marker,
the one he threw in among the others,
was not designed to help him not get picked.
It was no lump of moistened clay, no,
but a light one which would be the first

out of the crested helmet. Yes, Ajax
was the one who did these things, and I,
the slave whose mother was a foreigner,   1560
was there beside him.¹ You miserable man,
where are your eyes when you go on like this?   [1290]
Do you not realize your father's father,
ancient Pelops, was a barbarian,
who came from Phrygia? And Atreus,
the man who spawned you, wasn't he the one
who prepared that sacrilegious dinner,
and served up his own brother's children as a meal
for him to eat?² And then, as for yourself,
the mother who bore you came from Crete.   1570
And her own father caught her having sex,
screwing some stranger. He abandoned her
to be killed in silence by a bunch of fish.³
That's the kind of man you are. How can you
insult a man like me about my origins?
I am a son of Telamon, who won
my mother as his consort, his own prize   [1300]
for being the army's finest warrior.
She was of royal blood, Laomedon's daughter,
the most desirable of all the battle spoils.   1580
Alcmene's son gave her to Telamon.⁴

¹In the *Iliad*, the Achaeans chose a warrior to answer Hector's challenge to single combat by lottery. Some warriors voluntarily put their tokens in a helmet, the helmet was shaken up, and the warrior whose lot fell out first was chosen (in this case it was Ajax's token). The reference to the lump of moistened clay refers to the practice of putting in an exceptionally heavy marker, which had less chance of falling out first.

²The two brothers Atreus and Thyestes had quarrelled. Atreus invited Thyestes to a dinner of reconciliation and there served him his own children to eat. Thyestes ate them without knowing what he was doing. Atreus then revealed what he had done.

³Agamemnon's mother, Aerope, was a daughter of Catreus, a descendant of the royal family of Crete. The sexual exploit mentioned resulted in her being sent away to be killed by drowning, but she was instead given to Atreus as his wife.

⁴Alcmene's son is Hercules, who went with Telamon to attack Troy in an earlier expedition. Laomedon was king of Troy.

63

Since I am nobly born and my parents
are both noble, too, how could I disgrace
my own flesh and blood? Ajax is lying here,
overcome by all his troubles, and you—
aren't you ashamed to say you'll toss him out
without a burial? Well, think of this—
if you just throw him out, along with him
you'll be casting off three more as well.
It's a finer thing for men to see me die   1590   [1310]
while labouring hard on his behalf
than fighting for your woman—or should I say
your brother's wife? Given what I've said,
don't think about my safety; look to your own.
For if you make things difficult for me,
you're going to wish you had been more afraid
and not quite so bold when you confronted me.

[Enter ODYSSEUS alone]

CHORUS LEADER
Lord Odysseus, you've come just in time,
if you're here to calm things, not make them worse.

ODYSSEUS
My friends, what's going on? From a long way off   1600
I heard the sons of Atreus shouting out
over this brave man's body.

AGAMEMNON
                    Lord Odysseus,
we have had to listen for far too long   [1320]
to the most shameful language from this man.
Is that not reason enough?

ODYSSEUS
                    Well, let's see—
I could forgive a man who had been listening
to someone else who was abusing him
and who then joined in a war of insults.

AGAMEMNON

I did insult him, because his actions
were a direct affront to me.

ODYSSEUS

                        What did he do   1610
to injure you?

AGAMEMNON

                    He says he will not let
this corpse remain without a burial.
He'll set it in a grave, no matter what I do.

ODYSSEUS

Well, may someone who's a friend of yours
speak his mind and still remain a colleague
the way he was before?

AGAMEMNON

                    You should speak out.   [1330]
I would scarcely be thinking properly
if I said no. Among the Argives
I consider you my greatest friend.

ODYSSEUS

Then listen. In deference to the gods   1620
don't be so unyielding you throw Ajax out
without a burial. You should not let
that spirit of violence at any time
seize control of you, not to the extent
that you then trample justice underfoot.
This man became my greatest enemy
in all our army on that very day
I beat him for the armour of Achilles.
But for all the man's hostility to me,
I would not disgrace him. Nor would I deny   1630
that in my view he was the finest warrior   [1340]
among the Argive men who came to Troy,
after Achilles. So if you dishonour him,
you would be unjust. It would not harm him,
but you'd be contravening all those laws
the gods established. When a good man dies,

it is not right to harm him, even though
he may be someone you hate.

AGAMEMNON
                              Odysseus,
you mean you're arguing against me,
on his behalf?

ODYSSEUS
                    Yes, that's what I mean.   1640
I did hate him, when it was all right to hate.

AGAMEMNON
Why would you not walk all over him,
now that he's dead?

ODYSSEUS
                    Son of Atreus,
do not take pleasure in advantages
which are dishonourable.

AGAMEMNON
                    An all-powerful king   [1350]
does not show reverence all that easily.

ODYSSEUS
But he can give out honourable rewards
to friends when they advise him prudently.

AGAMEMNON
A good man should obey those in command.

ODYSSEUS
Why not concede? You'll still be in control,   1650
although you let your friends prevail against you.

AGAMEMNON
Just remember the kind of man he was,
the one for whom you want to do this favour.

ODYSSEUS
The man was an enemy of mine, that's true.
But he was once a noble warrior.

66

AGAMEMNON
Why are you doing this? Why such respect
for the dead body of an enemy?

ODYSSEUS
His excellence moves me to do it,
far more than his hostility to me.

AGAMEMNON
Men who act the way you're doing now   1660
are unreliable.

ODYSSEUS
                    Let me assure you,
among human beings most are changeable,
sometimes friendly, then sometimes bitter.

AGAMEMNON
Are those the sort of men you'd recommend   [1360]
that we accept as friends?

ODYSSEUS
                    Well, I wouldn't recommend
we choose someone inflexible.

AGAMEMNON
                         All right,
but now you'll make us look like cowards.

ODYSSEUS
No. Every Greek will think we're being just.

AGAMEMNON
So you would urge me to give my permission,
and let this corpse receive a burial?   1670

ODYSSEUS
I would. For I myself will someday reach
the state he's in, as well.

AGAMEMNON
                    There we have it.
All men work to benefit themselves.

ODYSSEUS

    For whom should I make such an effort
    if not for myself?

AGAMEMNON

                We'll have to announce
    that you're the one responsible for this,
    not me.

ODYSSEUS

          However you do it, it will serve
    to bring you all kinds of advantages.

AGAMEMNON

    Well, in any case, you can rest assured   [1370]
    I would grant you a greater favour   1680
    than this burial. As for this man here,
    down in the underworld he is my enemy,
    just as he was on earth. But you can do
    whatever you think is appropriate.

[AGAMEMNON and his escort leave]

CHORUS LEADER

    Given how you have acted here today,
    Odysseus, any man who now asserts
    that you are not by nature wise is stupid.

ODYSSEUS

    I now proclaim that from this moment on
    I am Teucer's friend, as much as earlier
    I was his enemy. And I am willing   1690
    to join with him in burying the dead,
    working with you and omitting nothing
    human beings may need to honour and respect   [1380]
    their finest warriors.

TEUCER

                Noble Odysseus,
    I have nothing but praise for what you've said.
    You have done so much to disprove my fears.
    Of all the Argives, you were the one
    who was his greatest enemy, and yet

you are the only one to stand by him,
to lend a helping hand. For when he died   1700
and you were still alive, you could not bear
to see such injuries inflicted on him,
not like that frantic general who was here.
He and his brother wanted their revenge
by casting Ajax off without a grave.
And so may our all-ruling father Zeus,
high on Olympus, the unforgiving Furies,   [1390]
and Justice, too, who fulfils all things,
destroy those evil men with evil deaths,
just as they tried to rid themselves of Ajax,   1710
outrageous treatment he did not deserve.
But you, child of venerable Laertes,
I hesitate to let you touch the corpse
in these funeral rites, for that may well offend
the man who died. But as for all the rest,
join in with us. If you wish, bring someone,
any soldier in the army will be welcome.
I must get all things ready. Odysseus,
you must know you've acted nobly for us.

ODYSSEUS
That's what I wished. But if you object   1720   [1400]
to my participation here with you,
I'll defer to what you want and leave.

[ODYSSEUS leaves]

TEUCER
Enough. Too much time has passed already.
Hurry now. Some of you scoop out a hollow grave,
others set the cauldron high up on the stand,
with fire all around, so we can start
the ritual cleansing promptly. One of you,
bring from his hut the armour he would wear
behind his shield. And you, too, my child,
since he's your father, use those loving arms   1730   [1410]
with all the strength you have and help me lift him.
His windpipe is still warm, and from it flows
his own dark spirit. Come then, come all of you

69

who say your are our friends, come quickly,
move out, and with your efforts honour Ajax.
There was no one to match his excellence.[1]
No nobler man has received such honour.

CHORUS
I know of many things which mortal men
can see and learn from. But until he meets it,
no one sees what is to come or his own fate.   1740   [1420]

[They all leave, bearing the body of Ajax.]

---

[1]The phrase which follows in the Greek reads "I mean, when he was living," which
deflates the tribute considerably. For that reason a number of editors have rejected
it as spurious. I have followed their lead and omitted the words.

A NOTE ON THE TRANSLATOR

Ian Johnston is an emeritus professor at Vancouver Island University, Nanaimo, British Columbia, Canada. He is the author of *The Ironies of War: An Introduction to Homer's Iliad* and has translated a number of classic works into English, including the following (most of them published as books and ebooks by Richer Resources Publications).

Aeschylus, *Oresteia*
Aeschylus, *Persians*
Aeschylus, *Prometheus Bound*
Aeschylus, *Seven Against Thebes*
Aeschylus, *Suppliant Women*
Aristophanes, *Birds*
Aristophanes, *Clouds*
Aristophanes, *Frogs*
Aristophanes, *Knights*
Aristophanes, *Lysistrata*
Aristophanes, *Peace*
Cuvier, *Discourse on Revolutionary Upheavals on the Surface of the Earth*
Descartes, *Discourse on Method*
Descartes, *Meditations on First Philosophy*
Diderot, *D'Alembert's Dream and Rameau's Nephew*
Euripides, *Bacchae*
Euripides, *Electra*
Euripides, *Medea*
Euripides, *Orestes*
Homer, *Iliad*
Homer, *Odyssey*
Kafka, *Metamorphosis, A Hunger Artist, In the Penal Colony, and Other Stories*
Kant, *On Perpetual Peace*
Kant, *Universal History and Nature of the Heavens*
Lamarck, *Zoological Philosophy, Volume I*
Lucretius, *On the Nature of Things*
Nietzsche, *Birth of Tragedy*
Nietzsche, *Beyond Good and Evil*
Nietzsche, *Genealogy of Morals*
Nietzsche, *On the Uses and Abuses of History*
Ovid, *Metamorphoses*
Rousseau, *Discourse on the Sciences and the Arts*
Rousseau, *Discourse on the Origins of Inequality*
Rousseau, *Social Contract*
Sophocles, *Ajax*
Sophocles, *Antigone*
Sophocles, *Oedipus at Colonus*
Sophocles, *Oedipus the King*
Sophocles, *Philoctetes*

Ian Johnston has a web site (at http://records.viu.ca/~johnstoi/) where he has posted these translations, as well as a number of lectures, workbooks, essays, and book reviews.